Let's Take This Offline

Ana Maria Dorevich

Published by Ana Maria Dorevich, 2024.

Table of Contents

PREFACE

Ana Maria Dorevich (née Monteiro)

Welcome to my personal journey as a career Administrator. With over thirty-five years of experience, working in various industries, I have not only perfected many aspects of my profession but have learned many life-long lessons along the way. I hope to share some of those experiences with you, and hope my book has a positive effect...and perhaps makes you smile in the process.

This book is more geared towards your career as an EA on the whole, and not what your day to day tasks look like nor how you should manage them. I am hoping that if you are looking to become an Administrator, that you already have plans for your education and/or some form of experience on-hand. I hope my tips and life lessons will guide you to making informed decisions in your own career, and a give you a small taste of what you may encounter. The good, the bad and the ugly.

Despite what many might think, being any type of Assistant is an integral part of all companies (big or small) and crucial to the success of the executive(s) you might support. There are various steps, transitions and growth opportunities along the way that will lead to a successful and fulfilling career. To some extent, you will also experience challenges, conflicting personalities, and even unacceptable behaviour but we will delve into that, and their positive solutions, throughout the various chapters ahead.

I have had the privilege of many influential teachers and coaches throughout my career, and more recently have gained a few proteges of my own. It's very humbling and inspiring to know that I can pass on my knowledge and experience to those who now take the reins in an administrative role. I hope your journey is as gratifying as mine has been.

CHAPTER 1
First-Things-First (Education and Foot in the Door)

So what do you want to be when you grow up? Something we were either asked or in the least thought about in our earlier years. When nearing the end of our high school tribulations, it started to get real. For me it didn't take much thought. Either become a fashion designer and move to Paris or get my pilot's license. In the end, I choose computer science. A realistic choice for me at the time, and one that had me realize (in part) my first two choices in the future. Due to the good fortune I have had during my career, I was able to secure a position with an airline and traveled to Paris, where I enjoyed visiting all the museums and fashion houses. Years later I also had the opportunity to pilot a Cessna aircraft (alongside a licensed pilot). In essence, I met all my goals by that time.

Computer Science was a smart and natural choice for me. Being somewhat of a geek and a sci-fi lover, I relished the thought of operating a computer. When I first signed up for the program, I was a teenager in the eighties. There were no home computers, and only large mainframes at a handful of companies. Most of my classes consisted of middle-aged women who, up to that point, had only used typewriters and steno pads at their respective offices. They were very intimidated with all the hardware and software, but I jumped right in. I was like a kid in a candy store and enjoyed every minute.

I attended school on a part-time basis, as I worked in retail full-time to earn a living. Due to the part time status, it took me longer to complete the program but it started me on my career path. One that I would not change, even if I could. By the time I received my diploma, not only had I already worked in two office environments (a national bank and an airline) but I was married with a baby on the way. Over the course of the following seven years, I continued my career and grew my family ~ having two more children. Three in total by the time I was thirty-five.

Nowadays, most young adults were born into the computer age and have always been exposed to them. Knowing how to operate a computer and various software applications is second nature. With the addition of smart phones and various other technologies that have facilitated ease of organizing, communicating, and socializing, it has made my job a lot easier as well. But being an Administrator of any type isn't just about the tech advances, although helpful overall. What I would suggest in this day and age would be a college or university degree in Business Administration, Communications and/or Project Management for the budding new Admin. In fact, many corporations note a degree of some type (or extensive hands-on experience) as a prerequisite on their job postings for any administrative opportunities.

Regardless of our age or the era we grew up in, educating ourselves is important. Whether it be attaining a formal education or learning through hands on training. We also learn from our peers, our superiors and our subordinates. Having been born and raised in Toronto, Canada, I was lucky enough to have various options to start and grow my career. When it came to the educational establishment I choose, I wasn't loyal to any one school but instead was selective with what program they offered and what I could personally gain from it. In addition, I spoke with career Executive Assistants at that time, and gained valuable insight into software applications that they were using. In other words, I did my research and it paid off.

Over the years, and with technology constantly advancing, adapting to new software was part and parcel of my growth. Similar to most careers, you need to stay current or you will fall behind. Every time a new software package or version of such came out, I hopped on a training course. Not because I had to but because I wanted to. You need to steer your own path for your own benefit. Although most companies provide required and even recurrent training in some areas, they also offer other educational opportunities. Some even cover the costs, or at least in part will reimburse you for such.

Don't forget all the soft skills you gain and maintain throughout your life that can be implemented into your career. These soft skills are often unintentionally used in our day-to-day work scenarios. For me it was having three children and needing to be super organized at home. These skills poured over into my administrative roles and were crucial with my successfully maintaining various aspects of my job. Such as calendar management, multitasking, and prioritizing. Soft skills can be gained in various ways and not just by having a growing family. Servicing your car regularly, maintaining a garden, volunteering with various charities, etc. We all learn soft skills during our lifetime.

What are some other skills that are required to be a successful Executive Assistant you might ask? There are many that would be advantageous but in naming a few, I would suggest time management, conflict resolution, leadership skills, business operations, accounting, customer service, human resource, event management, emotional intelligence (EI), procurement management, and many more. Many of these offerings would be included in a college or university degree but I completed them separately throughout my career. Just a few years ago, I was lucky enough to get certified as an Advanced Executive Assistant (ACEA). Long story short, it doesn't happen overnight but you start small and dream big.

What happens when you're still in school but want a related job where you can gain experience? I would suggest getting an entry-level position, preferably in administration but something that will get your foot in the door. Before completing my college program, I was a data entry clerk when I first started in an office environment. You will gain hands-on experience, and this will just add to your resume. I can't say enough about learning on-the-job. I would also suggest that being picky is not an option when you start your first role. That old saying "beggars can't be choosers" stands true when getting your foot in the door as a junior employee. All the perks and knowledge will come in time.

Be humble. Ask a lot of questions. Learn from others. Take notes. Build your network. Work hard!

CHAPTER 2
The Negotiator (Offers, Salary, Promotions and Opportunities)

Did you know that the minimum wage in the province of Ontario in 1985 was $3.85? Granted, the cost of living was more affordable but we didn't earn much at the end of the day. Today in 2023, it has increased to $16.65.

When you get that initial Admin job offer and review your benefits, including salary, understand that it is negotiable. Don't be afraid to counter with proposals. If the offer is for an entry-level position, or more so a unionized clerical role, don't be surprised if they are unable to adjust the offer. Specifically with unionized positions, as they are bound to collective agreements and have fixed pay scales. Unionized employees eventually go up in pay scale over time, and with seniority, but once they reach the top level, that's the cap and it can't be changed until a new collective agreement is put in place. I was a unionized Administrative Assistant for ten years when I worked for an airline, and to be honest I enjoyed it very much. Enjoying your role isn't always reliant on money. You need to take into consideration all the other perks and benefits that the company has to offer. With the airline, I had discounted flights for myself and my family. Health benefits and location were also excellent. Although I paid union dues during this time, the pros greatly outweighed the cons.

There have also been a few occasions where I have taken a pay cut when starting a new job. Again, it's not always about the money. Leaving a company where the commute was terrible, and starting with a new company closer to home, is considered a positive move too. Even though I took a pay cut, I saved money in not commuting as far and also had more time with my family. You need to consider your own situation and what works best for you when reviewing and accepting a job offer. Even when initially looking for a new opportunity. Consider all the aspects and ensure it's what you really want.

Do not be discouraged by your initial income when first starting your career. We have all been in that position. Pay increases and promotions take time, and you will gain the respect of your peers and managers if you are open to learning and working hard. Patience is a virtue, they say. Aside from gaining recognition, there is also the possibility of attaining a promotion. Depending on the company and their practices, promotions (including title changes) are occasionally offered when warranted. Nothing happens overnight, however. You need to prove yourself and show your worth. Don't be shy to offer to take on more responsibility too or work on special projects. In doing so, you not only show your value but you learn from working on new initiatives for your team or manager.

What if I've been in the same administrative role for a long time and haven't been recognized? This is a question that we often ask ourselves but it is one that we should own. If you are not content in your current role due to lack of recognition (or any other reason), then you have to review your own options. Do not put the owkness or blame on anybody else. Firstly, you can approach your manager and be honest with them. Ask them if there is any imminent opportunity for growth within your current role. Unfortunately, and depending on the company's practices, your manager may take you seriously or not. At one of the companies I worked for, I was promised promotions, title and salary change during my initial interview. After seven years of approaching my manager, and receiving disappointing lip service, this never came to fruition. There were a lot of broken promises, employee favouritism and unfortunately a misogynistic stance by my manager and most of his senior team. It was at that point that I resigned and found other employment. Ironically, I ended up securing an Executive Assistant position within a technology company where I earned substantially more. Everything happens for a reason sometimes.

Another benefit of being patient as related to your salary and promotions is that you build confidence over time, not just knowledge. This is something that will be very beneficial but it's not really something you can learn from a textbook. Your experience will gain momentum and you start learning more, experiencing more, appreciating more. You also start opening your eyes more to what you want from your administrative career, and definitely what you do not nor will tolerate. In my own career as an Executive Assistant, I have found that the benefits of time have far outweighed the negative challenges. You will have ups and downs but always remember that you are your own boss and you ultimately make the hard stop decisions where your career is concerned.

The bottom line is that good things come to those who wait. Review all your options, no matter how much experience you have. In the end, we don't know if the opportunity will fill all our expectations until we start. After that, we take one day at a time. Keep building your knowledge base and networking skills. There are various social media websites for career oriented individuals, such as LinkedIn, where you can start growing your circle, sign up for courses, search for jobs and share your experience with companies and recruiters. If you prioritize and look at yourself as your own, individual company, you will be in a better position to find the perfect administrative role for you. That role will hopefully offer all that you want and need. And that need may change over time but that's ok. Always have a basic plan, even if the plan changes. You can still set your priorities, speak up regarding job offers, salary expectations and other benefits. Most companies need you more than you need them. Always be your number one fan, your number one priority and showcase your strengths.

Be selective. Be patient. Be Confident.

CHAPTER 3
Who's The Boss? (360 Approaches, Interviewing the Interviewer, Compatibility)

As an Executive Assistant, or in any other administrative-type role, who you report to is very important. Sometimes you may report to one senior leader but support another (or various others and their teams). You get a first glimpse of your perspective boss when you have your initial interview with them. As much as they are interviewing you, you too are interviewing them. I would say that most people are a good judge of character but you don't really know how your relationship will flourish (if at all) during that initial interview stage. If you are meeting the boss, then the company already felt that you were qualified. The main reason for having a one-on-one with your future manager (typically a second or third interview) is to gauge if you will be a good fit or not. I have always felt that this perspective works both ways, so don't be nervous. They too are being judged.

Should I be interviewing my perspective boss as they are interviewing me? Absolutely! At some point of most interviews, candidates always have the opportunity to ask questions. If you're fortunate enough to get a chance to speak directly to the individual you will be supporting, make sure you have a list of questions on-hand. The following are just a few examples of questions you should ask, as well as some that would not be appropriate:

Appropriate questions to ask perspective boss:

1. What would be a typical day for you?

2. Is this opportunity a new position? If not, why is the role vacant?
3. What are your daily work hour expectations, and is this a virtual/onsite/hybrid opportunity?
4. When do you expect to fill the role, and do you have a proposed start date in mind?
5. Is there any travel involved with this role?
6. What is your preferred method of communication? Are company phones provided?
7. How long have you been with the company?
8. Can you tell me a little about your team and the department?
9. Do you work closely with other specific leaders?
10. In your perspective, what are the main priorities of this opportunity?

Inappropriate questions to ask perspective boss:

1. What is the salary/bonus/benefits' situation?
2. Can I take vacation any time of the year or are there any blackout dates?
3. Is there free parking in the building?
4. Is your team very big? I prefer to work alone.
5. What type of perks do we get at this company?

All of the above noted appropriate questions to ask show interest and are legitimate questions to be directed specifically at your perspective boss. 1. Inquiring about their daily nuances is good to know for your own benefit, and they will like the fact that you asked. 2. Asking why the role is vacant is mostly beneficial for you. If there is a high turnover in the role? There could be a negative reason for that; however, if the previous Assistant was promoted or retired, then it not only shows longevity in the role but the possibility for advancement. 3) Knowing what the onsite situation is, under the current climate, would be beneficial to know. I would try to follow their lead and work the same pattern as them (as I do with my current employer). 4. Asking about the timeline and when they expect a new Executive Assistant to start is a valid question. It also give you time to tie-up loose ends if you're transitioning from another role and have to give two weeks' notice. 5. Often times there may be travel involved in your role (in local area or to another city), therefore another good question to ask. 6. Company phones are often provided to Executive Assistants, and therefore it's always good to inquire. Some companies provide them and some do not (but will reimburse a portion of personal mobile device costs). 7. Asking about their history with the company also shows interest, and it's a fact that most people like to speak of their own accomplishments (especially a perspective boss). 8. Getting information about the leader's team and department on the whole is a great way to find out how big the team is, and if you will possibly be supporting them to some extent too. 9. If your leader works closely with other lateral leaders, then you will have the opportunity to communicate with their Executive Assistants too. This also gives you an idea of the size of his work connections and possible responsibilities prior to starting. 10. Asking about the main priorities of the opportunity gives you a snapshot into his main requirements of your role. For example, calendar management, travel and expense reporting. Not all leaders are the same. Some prefer to manage their own calendar, while others do not. These tips are a good way to get some insight into your perspective boss' world, the role and the future responsibilities.

As for the above noted 'inappropriate' questions to ask, these should be directed to either Human Resource or the company Recruiter. These questions will be frowned up, compared to the other more productive questions also mentioned above.

During this interview, and while asking all the noted questions, you will get a feel for the individual's personality, worth ethics and priorities of the role. It is important that you are comfortable and compatible, and although this is difficult to truly decipher in a short period of time, the more communication you have the more insight you will walk away with. Remember, the choice is ultimately yours. Who you report to and/or support is very important as an Executive Assistant. As the company decides on you as a candidate, you too have a decision to make.

Often times the individual we weren't sure of turns out to be a truly great boss. Although sometimes the opposite occurs, and we are surprised by their negative approach once hired. Again, the decision is yours. Whether to accept the opportunity (or not) and ultimately be happy or move on if it doesn't work out the way you anticipated. My only rule of thumb is never to leave a job without having another one lined up. This can sometimes be frustrating but it's the best stance to take.

Always be prepared and professional!

CHAPTER 4
Can We Talk? (Communication and Interpersonal Skills)

What does communication mean to you? I don't think I have enough time to write about every aspect of general communication but will do my best to speak to its benefits as far as being an Executive Assistant.

Communication has probably been in the top three of priorities my entire career. In one way or another, we all communicate in some form (even without words, such as body language). When it comes to my role, communicating with your leader and any others you support is (or should be) your main priority. You cannot have a successful relationship with your boss, nor others, without productive communication. You cannot just assume certain things without the facts. Without asking, you may be making errors that will have various repercussions.

Communication is key to an Executive Assistant's role. You need to ask questions, and then ask them again. But it works both ways. People often work at different paces, which can hinder the intent and desired outcome of good communication. You've been given a task and deadline by your boss. You've done your part and reached out to all the players for feedback. Only two out of ten have responded. What do you do? I have always been a true believer in if I'm asking the team (in this scenario) for feedback, then it's really my boss who's asking. I once had a former boss ask me for the names of all team members who had not responded, and she dealt with them. This is poor communication on their part. There are only so many requests and reminders you can send as an Assistant before the fault falls on them. But it can put you in a bad light as well. In certain situations, with absent responses, I started copying my boss on all emails. It sometimes becomes necessary to do this, although it's not my first choice of communication. I don't believe our leaders need to be included in day to day communication but sometimes it's necessary.

Good communication also includes relationships with your peers, including other Executive Assistants. It's a crucial part of scheduling joint meetings or events, in addition to general information exchanges. We learn so much from our peers, and perhaps share our own knowledge with them as well.

I have also had the opportunity (within my Assistant role) of managing employee communication, which reached thousands of employees. Using various forms of software and media, such as CCTV monitors and communicating information on a wide scale. It was actually a part of my role at the time that enjoyed most. As an amateur photographer, I included those skills to capture various employee events and post those photos for all to enjoy. It gave me great pleasure receiving feedback from employees about the photos or upcoming events, merely because of communicating those details to them.

Whether official communication is part of your role or not, always keep the door open for questions and answers. It's just another way we learn and grow within our administrative career. A quick email, phone call or personal visit to a colleague can give you all the answers you need. Don't be afraid to approach your boss either with questions. If you want to do your job right, asking questions is key. Also encourage others to do the same. Tell them not to hesitate to contact you if they have any concerns or feedback.

So what does a lack of communication as an Executive Assistant look like? Missing information on reports. Missed flights. Inaccurate expense claims. Events scheduled on wrong dates. It can be quite catastrophic without using clear and concise communication, and it will reflect poorly on you.

It is also important that you are clear with your own communication. Sometimes there is miscommunication when somebody relays information to you but other times it's the reverse. We can't help the occasional human error but if we practice good communication skills, it lowers the chances of that happening. I always try to document my communication by sending an email, as opposed to a quick phone call. This way you have a paper trail and can refer to it as required. I very rarely delete any of my emails but instead keep them for future reference. This also gives you the opportunity to write all the details of your request clearly and ask the recipient to confirm as well.

How do I communicate face-to-face with people if I'm a little timid? Interpersonal skills are another important part of being an Executive Assistant. We often write emails and sit back to see if/ when we get a response but communicating with our boss, team and colleagues in person is also, if not more, important. Administrators need to have that type of personality, the confidence and skill to approach people in person when required. Even if we have already sent an email, it's a good idea and beneficial to visit the recipient at their desk or office. In fact, you might get the answer(s) you're looking for quicker if you do this. In fact, I think it's more widely respected to do so, if possible. You may have some team members that are not situated in your location but for those that are, I would encourage communicating in person. If you have worked with these individuals for some time, there is no need to feel uncomfortable. Just ensure they do not look occupied when you approach them. You can always return if they look like they may be in a meeting or call.

You will slowly but surely build a good and solid relationship with all those you communicate with and will eventually grow your circle even more. It's a great opportunity to learn from others and share your knowledge with them as well. More importantly, it's the best and most productive way to manage your responsibilities and those of your team. Your boss will soon notice this, as will others that you regularly work with.

Communication works for those who work at it.

CHAPTER 5
Let Them Eat Cake (Event Management, Catering Meetings & Conferences)

Executive Assistants are responsible for various tasks, and have many duties but scheduling is probably one of the most important and constant. Whether it's managing various executive calendars, arranging conferences or event management and related catering. A big part of meetings and events usually includes some form of catering but what exactly does that entail? How many guests will there be? Which venue have you selected? Are there any dietary restrictions?

If you are arranging catering for a small group, let's make sure you gather all the details you need. First you will need to confirm the headcount. When sending out an invitation (via your business calendar or an online option), you have a basic idea of how many guests are invited but how many will actually attend is a different story. Sometimes you need to chase people in order to get their RSVP. If using your business calendar, such as Microsoft Outlook, you may have the ability to include voting buttons in your invite. You can customize these buttons so that guests can respond with more detail than just their RSVP, such as dietary restrictions. Once you have a general idea of your event headcount, you can start researching options for venue.

If you are still entertaining a small group and have the option of meeting rooms in your general area, then ensure you reserve a room well in advance in order to secure the space. Depending on your own personal scenario, you may or may not have various options for conference facilities. You should also ensure the space has any and all requirements you might need for your event, such as space for catering set up. If room reservations are managed by another team or individual, work closely with them to secure a room that not only fits all your needs but that is available. The location of the room is also important, and that it is convenient for guests on the day of the event/meeting.

Now that you have a perspective on the headcount and have secured an appropriate meeting room, you need to find a caterer. Although some companies have their own onsite catering available, it is not that common. Look for restaurants / caterers in your general area and check their menus. Most menus are available online in pdf format that you can download for future reference. Some caterers require ample time for requests, so make sure you approach them well in advance. Although for a smaller group, it may not be required. Ensure that you include all the dietary restrictions of your guests and be specific. If possible, ask them to label individual special orders with guest's name. Some restaurants will do this so there is no confusion.

Whether you are ultimately attending the meeting or not, always make sure you are present before it begins to ensure the catering is received and set up appropriately. It is important to confirm you received all that was ordered and that it is presented accordingly for the guests.

Well, that takes care of smaller meetings but what if you're approached to manage an event with two hundred guests? I have organized a few of those, and it's not as difficult as you might think. As long as you follow the basic steps you generally use for smaller events, you should have a general plan for larger ones.

For a large event you need to start researching hotels or possibly banquet facilities. You will need to contact the hotel directly and arrange an in-person meeting with their event coordinator (most hotels and banquet facilities will be happy to meet with you to discuss details and provide a tour if you're not already familiar with the venue). In most cases, larger venues will have a few fixed menus for bigger groups and also offer the option to customize these set menus as well. They typically charge a dollar amount per person, per item or package. Depending on your requirement (buffet or sit-down dinner), the venue will take all the required precautions to fit your needs. I have found them all to be very accommodating.

When arranging a larger venue, you will also need to consider other aspects, such as audio and visual requirements. One screen or two? Podium and microphone? Video capabilities or just audio? Most large venues have in-house audio/visual teams that can be hired for your function. Alternately you may want to choose your own external company but working with the venue directly for all your needs is most convenient. In addition to these requirements, venues can also provide various extras such as stationery for each table (notepads, pens, etc.). Usually this is offered at no cost. If you bring any external items to the venue, ask the event coordinator if it's permitted first. Items such as banners, posters, company swag, etc. If permitted, you can request a table for any giveaways to be set on.

Whether you choose to hold your larger event at a hotel or banquet facility, there will probably be a contract involved. You need to ensure that the contract is accurate before signing. The venue will usually hold off on finalizing the contract until the final headcount is confirmed, at which time they will want the contract signed – and possibly a deposit. If you do not have the authority to sign a contract (although most Executive Assistants do) just have your manager or senior director sign it for you. Make sure you use a corporate credit card for any and all payments. If you do not have your own corporate card, then ask your manager or senior director for this as well.

Similar to smaller meetings, larger events require that you arrive early before all the guests. Whether you are participating in the event or not, you need to ensure that everything is set up the way it was promised and outlined in the contract. In addition to day-of responsibilities, you may possibly be required to prepare other entities for the event - such as presentations, agendas, menu cards, name badges, etc. Always be prepared and meticulous with your plans, and you will always have successful events. Big or small.

Attention to detail is key for all catering / event coordination.

CHAPTER 6
My Liaisons (Building & Managing Relationships: Colleagues, Vendors, Clients)

As an Executive Assistant, how do you build, keep and grow relationships in a working environment? I would suggest that like personal relationships, it takes time to get to know somebody well but it initially just takes some effort to make that first move. Let's say you just started working for a new company as an Executive Assistant. You have most likely met your boss and the leadership team but what's just as crucial is getting to know other Executive Assistants.

Whether you support one senior executive or more than one, chances are there are various other senior leaders in the company that have their own Executive Assistant. Building a rapport with your counterparts is very important and will only work to your advantage in the end. You not only learn from other Administrators but they may eventually learn from you as well. You build your relationships with them and help each other along the way. You may also bounce ideas on them, and vice versa. Often times your leaders will meet and schedules will need to be cross referenced for availability. If you have a positive working relationship with your colleagues, it makes the process much better.

Building relationships with your counterparts is not the only relationships that are important, however. Getting to know your immediate team and their direct reports is also essential. These are people you will work with every day to some measure and building a rapport with all of them will be very beneficial. In addition, get to know as many other colleagues as possible throughout the organization – in various departments. Human Resources, Marketing, Accounting, Technology, etc. The more contacts / relationships you have, the easier it will be for you to manage your work and successfully support your leader.

On a more human level, having good working relationships support your mental health and all it has to offer. Positive relationships build confidence, motivation, and a sense of community. We are more productive in the workplace when all the pieces of the puzzle actually fit and get along. It's a basic need to feel connected, especially when working 'in-person' with our peers. During the pandemic (and possibly for other reasons), many of us endured long periods of virtual meetings. Any type of positive communication is productive and healthy (in person or virtual) but for me personally, I believe that nothing beats the old practice of talking with your peers by the 'water cooler', attending social gatherings and just communicating face-to-face. There is a reason for this. Firstly, body language and physical interaction is important. Shaking somebody's hand for example. Passing somebody in a hallway and saying hello, or just making some eye contact. Secondly, it can boost morale and even your career development. I worked 'in-person' the majority of my career, and never thought twice about it. Working from home, as an Executive Assistant, would be unheard of pre-pandemic.

Another great aspect of building relationships with your peers is that you may form some great friendships in the process. When you work closely with your peers, you get to know part of their personal lives as well (what we are willing to share) and find that we are all more alike than we know. I myself have met some great people throughout my career. Past and present friendships that were built on solid working relationships.

How about external business relationships you create and build as an Executive Assistant? As mentioned in past chapters, you will deal with various vendors for different reasons. From booking venues to catering requirements. You will also need to book travel, accommodations, private limos, etc. As a previous Office Manager, I also worked with building managers and maintenance, ordered numerous flower and basket arrangements, and even designed corporate swag for event celebrations. These too, and more, are all external relationships you will build. People you will come to trust and turn to for all your business needs. You build these external relationships and you will see how it effects your role and the success of your team.

You learn to not only build working relationships but long-lasting relationships vendors. This will lead to much success for all your business dealings. These relationships are beneficial to your success as well as the vendors. A happy customer is a loyal repeat customer. This may even lead to you securing discounts, special attention and excellent customer service. Be honest and transparent with your business dealings and requirements as they arise.

Don't be afraid to speak frankly with your vendors and be specific about your expectations. In the end, some vendors require signed contracts; therefore it is important that you are both content with the outcome of the details and the service provided. If possible, avoid getting too many people involved in your plans. This may skew the results and cause miscommunication along the way.

Similar to your vendors, and colleagues, your professionalism should always be top-notch when it comes to clients. Whether you are communicating with them via email, phone or in person, your utmost care and attention should be presented. You are representing your organization with all of your communication, and ultimately in the professional relationships you build. It's not just an external customer visiting your office. You should meet and greet them in a cordial and friendly manner. I have built and sustained many working relationships and can honestly say that it not only played a large part of my role and responsibility but was very gratifying on a professional level. Whether you are dealing with a building maintenance employee or the CEO of another company, you must treat them with the same respect and diplomacy. You shouldn't differentiate your treatment of others based on their position or hierarchy. In the end, you will be known for always being helpful and pleasant with all those that you work with, whether internal or external. Put your best foot forward, and you will always be recognized for the treatment of others.

Teamwork is the ability to work together toward a common vision successfully.

CHAPTER 7
Know Your Limits (Conflicts, Setbacks, Bullies & Harassment)

What do you do if you have a conflict with one of your colleagues? Firstly, it depends on the severity of the conflict. If it's something minor, I would suggest you try to resolve it directly with that individual. Communication is key to any relationship, business or personal. Always be humble, honest and friendly. Secondly, if the issue is more severe, then you should approach your boss. Check your company policies on any procedures regarding this but speaking with your senior leader is best. If you have any serious issues and/ or the concern involves your boss, then speak directly with Human Resources. Oddly enough, I have actually had a couple of bad experiences with former bosses and Human Resources directly, including favouritism, and even bullying – but I left those companies long ago.

There is no place for any type of harassment (nor violence) in the workplace. In fact, this is illegal. As noted in the *Occupational Health and Safety Act (OHSA)* of Ontario, Canada; "Workplace harassment can include unwelcome and/or repeated words or actions that are known or should be known to be offensive, embarrassing, humiliating or demeaning to a worker or group of workers". This Act also includes sexual harassment and workplace violence definitions. Individual organizations may also have additional workplace policies in place that include the above noted references, and sometimes even more.

Another area of contention is discrimination of any kind. As outlined in the *Ontario Human Rights Commission (OHRC)*, this includes [but is not limited to] discrimination of age, sexual orientation, race, and religion. I would suggest you learn about your rights, provincially and within your specific organization, and become fully educated on all aspects. Hopefully you will never encounter a toxic work environment but at least you will be aware of your rights.

How would you approach a situation where you were just not comfortable? Again, it all depends on the severity of the situation and your level of comfort. It may be a mere inconvenience (i.e. being voluntold to move to another department in order to accommodate another employee who is a friend of your manager). If that's the case, you need to weigh your options and priorities. I was in a similar situation and choose to remain with the organization simply because I enjoyed the role and company on the whole. However, it *did* cause tension in the future. After that, it just wasn't quite the same and I eventually choose to resign and find other employment. I will note that after I was displaced, in addition to other discrepancies, I approached Human Resources and they unfortunately sided with my manager. Just another incentive for me to resign. In the end, it was the best move I ever made.

Have you ever experienced a workplace bully in action? Although it's not a pretty sight (in any setting), it's interesting to see in a workplace environment. The assumption that they have more power or control than others is almost comical. If you are dealing with a colleague/lateral that is a bully, you have two choices. You can either accept the way they treat you (and others) or you can be diplomatic about it. Like my mother always used to say, "you get more flies with honey than you do vinegar". Ever since I have taken this stance, I have had no issues with workplace bullies. It's quite the scene watching a bully be deflated, or even be nice, once you use this approach. It has never failed me. But you *do* have to use some tact and confidence. A bully only continues bullying if nothing is said or done about it. How you control the situation is up to you and you only. Having said that, if the abuse is excessive you need to approach your superior. Don't ever be concerned about speaking up about any type of discomfort or more so harassment.

Another repercussion of workplace harassment (or abuse of power) is how it ultimately effects your position and any related setbacks you incur due to it. This is totally unacceptable. You go above and beyond in your role, you are always the first to help, and perhaps even overlook some minor issues because you really enjoy your job overall; but then you are stepped over for a position and somebody else gets a promotion. Favouritism is a sore spot for me, and one that I have personally been on the receiving end of a couple of times (on the negative end). Those that use their position of power, and perhaps even friendship, to show favouritism are very selfish and close minded. In fact, I have more respect for those leaders that overlook their 'friends' and award new opportunities to those that sincerely deserve them. Imagine that!

In a perfect world, there would be no issues, discomfort nor harassment of any type in the workplace or otherwise. Unfortunately there is always the opportunity of having a bad experience with a specific individual, group or organization altogether. These are aspects that you cannot possibly know when you have your first interview but it will be something you may experience over time. Always do what is best for you, what makes you comfortable and stay in a position where you can positively grow and work with decent individuals. For the most part, this has been the case for me. And when it wasn't, I either spoke up or eventually moved on to greener pastures.

Always put yourself first. Your mental health is your number one priority when it comes to these types of situations. In fact, working in a positive environment (where employees are respected and treated well) ensures a more productive workplace. I only wish that more companies (big and small) would take heed in that advice as well but for now I ask you to be your number one fan. Look out for yourself, your rights and even those around you – if you can. Some people are afraid to speak up and unfortunately end up enduring years of abuse (although it may not be considered that to some). If you feel it isn't right, it isn't right!

Self-care is a necessity. Make it a priority in your life and workplace.

CHAPTER 8
Let's get Personal (EA vs. PA)

Are you an Executive Assistant or a Personal Assistant? Is there a difference between the two? Both positions are very similar, only the EA supports senior leadership within an organization with various business requirements, whereas a PA also supports personal requests for those individuals outside a corporate office environment. In addition, many Personal Assistants work from their leader's homes. To be honest, the main difference in my perspective is merely geography. The needs of your executive or 'VIP' are not that dissimilar whether you are an Executive Assistant or Personal Assistant.

A Personal Assistant is a position designed to facilitate your life and assist by organizing your calendar and correspondence, and being a professional caretaker to efficiently structure your time. As a Personal Assistant, you will directly support executives for all their day-to-day needs, at home and/or business. This includes project coordination, travel schedules and being the main point of contact for the executive or in many cases their family.

Having said that, the role of an Executive Assistant is more tactical than a Personal Assistant. They are more involved in crucial decision making and providing valuable feedback. Whereas a Personal Assistant focuses more on managing daily tasks.

As related to required skills, there are no great variances either. You must pay attention to detail, have the ability to multitask, possess strong organizational skills, and display pristine communication, interpersonal and time management skills – among other proficiencies. It would also be ideal to have some measure of industry knowledge, depending on who you support. Whether you assist a doctor, lawyer or celebrity, having industry knowledge is beneficial and will enhance your relationship with your leader.

Similar to an Executive Assistant, you can earn your certification as a CPA (Certified Personal Assistant). The Association of Administrative Professionals offers the CCAP (Canadian Certified Administrative Professional) credential, whereas in the United States you can attain this through IAAP (International Association of Accessibility Professionals). Prior to this, it's best to attain your education in a formal program, such as a Business Management or Administrative Specialist diploma from an accredited institution.

As a Personal Assistant, you might need to include running personal errands for your boss, such as gift shopping, taking care of personal bills, bank runs, oversee household and landscaping services, just to name a few. Although I have never been a Personal Assistant myself, I have had some duties crossover in my career. Arranging tuxedo rentals, lunch pick-ups, family travel arrangements, consulate visits for Visa requests, etc. As a Personal Assistant, you may not earn as much as an Executive Assistant however. Depending on your employer and their requirements, that could change but the rule of thumb is that corporate assistants supporting executives will receive a higher salary.

How do you become a 'great' Assistant (Executive or Personal)? Know your leader's business, keep your boss informed, be prepared and proactive, and always own your mistakes. Being accountable is crucial for either role. Be advised that there is no standard job description for Personal Assistants, and the duties and responsibilities vary depending on who you will support. Your boss may ask you to go to the veterinary and pick up their pet snake one afternoon. Somewhat extreme, but you get the picture. There are often times that there is no set schedule as a PA, so don't expect a strict 9-5 job. You also have to prioritize and organize your boss' life, which doesn't always align with your own. You will need to plan around your own schedule to accommodate your boss' needs.

Don't get me wrong, being a Personal Assistant can be very fulfilling and you might work with wonderful individuals but choose your commitments carefully and have them be clear on your responsibilities beforehand. And it's ok to be or become friends with your boss but there will be a professional line in this relationship. Don't pry into their personal life unless they choose to share any details with you. Working that close together will enable you to learn a lot about your boss' personal life but do not comment or provide negative feedback, unless they encourage you to be honest with your opinion(s). Remember that they are still your boss.

Building a relationship with your boss will take time but as with most relationships, you will eventually be able to read their mind and be proactive with your duties and responsibilities. Discuss their expectations of you upfront, and ask a lot of questions when you first start in the role. You can even advise your boss that you will be very inquisitive at first in order to learn all that you need to be successful in your role. They will be thankful for that, and in the end so will you. If you are responsible for managing a home (especially somebody else's home) it is a great obligation. You may be responsible for paying all the bills each month, and discussing these requirements with your boss will not be necessary after time. There will be many things you will do in the background. I always said that an assistant is somebody who does many tasks so that their boss doesn't have to.

Regardless of your administrative role, the skills you develop over time will be the foundation you need to succeed and grow your career. Whichever route you choose to take, find an administrative position that you enjoy, are qualified for, and are comfortable with. If you are very junior, then start off as an Administrative or Personal Assistant, and take time to gain experience and knowledge. In the meantime, continue your education and when you're ready, you can consider a leap into an Executive Assistant or Chief of Staff opportunity. You will be ready. Just be patient in the meantime and appreciate the ride. Don't be so worried about the destination, and enjoy the journey.

"Assistants are the secret weapons of high achievers."

CHAPTER 9

Savoir-faire (Diplomacy, Tact and Confidentiality)

First and foremost, being an Executive Assistant requires a great deal of confidentiality in any capacity, any company, and with any leader you might support. In addition, confidentiality isn't secluded to what may be communicated verbally. It goes without saying that there are various steps to follow when keeping your work safe, including but not limited to protecting your passwords and screentime. Always set your computer to sleep mode when you are away from the area. Be careful when sharing information digitally as well, including any attachments you may send. These steps, and others, may even be official processes and procedures within your company (and perhaps even more). Always ensure you are fully aware of all rules your company may have that go above and beyond the standard safety protocols of keeping your work safe.

As related to verbal communication, always be tactful and careful with what information you share. I always stand by the rule that less is more. Whether I'm privy to upcoming organizational restructuring or where my boss is going on vacation with their family, this is not information that should be shared with anybody. As an Executive Assistant, you will be privy to a lot of confidential information but don't think it's specific to work-related topics only. You will be representing your senior leaders, in their presence or absence, therefore always be cognizant of this protect and their privacy.

When practicing confidentiality, are you being diplomatic? Do you know how to display diplomacy? How you communicate with others will aid in how you in turn are treated. Although displaying diplomacy and tact doesn't come naturally to everybody, it is something that you can definitely learn with time. Unfortunately

I have witnessed other Executive Assistants being quite rude to colleagues simply because they had information they wouldn't share with them. It's all about the delivery and how you treat people. You need to treat colleagues, of all levels, with the best customer service possible. Again, you are representing your senior leader(s), not to mention your own character.

How would you handle gossip in the office? For the most part throughout history, office gossip has been relatively harmless; however, it's not acceptable unless all accept it. Being secretive and spreading rumours about others is not only unprofessional but very inappropriate. As an Executive Assistant, I have actually experienced this firsthand, and sadly by other Executive Assistants. There was one occurrence when a group of Executive Assistants went out for lunch to a local restaurant, and one of them started talking about the personal lives of more than one of our leaders at the time. In great detail I might add. She mentioned various relationships they had (inside and outside work). And this Executive Assistant actually looked proud about how much 'dirt' she had on this individual, which was very embarrassing. This was so out of line that I was tempted to leave. The eye opener by the end of this get together was that as much as this Executive Assistant was talking about others, they could potentially talk about you behind your back as well. But if you are always honest with yourself and others, you won't get involved in such childish discussions.

Being tactful is also being professional in the workplace, as well as respectful of other people (and yourself). If you carry yourself in a certain way, others will see that and treat you accordingly. If you ever have a concern, however, don't be hesitant about approaching your manager directly or Human Resource. Don't ever be afraid of speaking up about people or situations that make you uncomfortable. At the end of the day, don't be part of the problem but instead a part of the solution.

There are also occurrences of toxic situations, and some that don't even pertain to you directly; but other administrators or colleagues might be having conflicts and it could affect your work and peace of mind in the office. You can try to do your best to stay out of it and focus on your own work, or be supportive. Sometimes people are going through hardships (personally or work related) that we are not aware of. This can have a domino effect and influence all that work around them. Be kind and approach your colleague. Ask if there is anything you can do to help them. We spend a lot of time with those we work with, so treat them with the same respect and care as you would a friend or family member that is going through a rough time.

Being tactful is not only about what you say to others but how you approach your colleagues as well. Try to gauge the personality of the person you are speaking with. You will find that some of your colleagues are very expressive and talkative, while others tend to be more on the quiet side. Be cognizant of this, and respectfully approach each person with tact and diplomacy. This will greatly help you build a solid relationship with those you work with on a day to day basis, and also build your reputation as a very diplomatic Executive Assistant. Help others with their wants and needs, and they will in turn help you with yours. Being kind goes a long way in this type of job, and I imagine in all careers.

I truly believe as an Executive Assistant that you need to naturally have a certain personality type to be successful to do your job well but again, there are various courses you can take on improving communication skills and how to work well with others. This applies to not only your colleagues but external customers as well. Don't forget about all the soft skills you might bring to the role too, including empathy, assertiveness and fairness. If you follow all company policies, protect your digital information, as well as other topics and conversations.

"Tact is the knack of making a point without making an enemy." — *Isaac Newton*

CHAPTER 10
Old Dog, New Tricks (Continuing Education)

You complete your formal education and enter the workforce. Not so fast! During my career I have continued my education at every opportunity. You will become stagnant and fall behind if you do not keep up with new processes. Whether it be new technologies, updates to existing programs or growth opportunities, we never stop learning new ideas that will only add value to our roles.

When I first started my career, most offices didn't even have computers onsite. They weren't mainstream at that time, hence my choice to study technology. Once I finished my program, I still did most things manually – although I started to see the odd desktop computer here-and-there. As this technology was new, as was I to its capabilities, it gave me the opportunity to learn even more hands-on in the workplace. I also found that different companies had different programs, which was somewhat of a challenge but gave me the opportunity to gain even more knowledge with varying software. Over the years, new software and/or versions were introduced. I always kept current with each update, which helped me to capitalize on my base training within each organization.

Learning new technological skills also expanded my resume and added to my already vast administrative experience. I learned how to create my own website (manually), which allowed me to update employee newsletters and other communications' platforms. Although not a typical Executive Assistant duty, it was of great interest to me. This not only enhanced my knowledge but motivated me to learn even more.

Parlez-vous francais? Hablas español? Are you bilingual? How do you feel about learning a new language? There are various administrative opportunities that require you to be bilingual. Most of these opportunities offer a higher salary, and can definitely increase your chances of finding a role that works to your advantage. Depending on the role(s), organization or location of your choice, it may be a great opportunity to expand your knowledge and secure a bilingual role. You will see this requirement in many government jobs.

How are your soft skills? What are my soft skills? As an Executive Assistant, you will most likely bring many natural soft skills to the table. This includes tact and diplomacy (as discussed in previous chapter), compassion and organizational skills, just to name a few. As a mother of three children, I learned to multitask very early on. These types of skills will transfer into your career and enhance your role. Although many soft skills *do* come naturally, there are options for learning these characteristics or in the very least, assist you in realizing potential you

You may also encounter required training within various organizations. This includes but is not limited to Code of Conduct, and Workplace Violence & Harassment or Occupational Health & Safety. There are no costs involved with this type of in-house training, and it's required by most companies (as a one-time offering or often times recurring). Many companies also have employee development sites on their Intranet which are available for all at no cost. They usually consist of single courses, short-term webinars or full programs.

Various companies will also cover the cost of external educational offerings if, for the most part, it is related to your current job or career goals. So if you want to take swimming lessons as an

Executive Assistant, the company will probably not cover that cost. Having said that, some companies have 'wellness' programs that you can take advantage of, which promote good health and a positive mindset. You may be entitled to a capped amount per year that you can use toward personal items or training that are focused on your physical and mental wellbeing. This too is a beneficial way of staying on top of things. You need to be healthy in all aspects in order to do your job well. This is a mandatory aspect to your role, and really for everybody. You can discuss all your employment offerings with your manager or Human Resource, and check your company Internet for more details as well. Stay informed in every way.

But even if your company does not cover the cost of external education, or not in full, do what you can to stay interested and educated in all that you do. Never think that it is a waste of time or money. You need to remain invested in yourself, more so than others. Over time you will not only become more knowledgeable but companies will see that you have the credentials and drive that perhaps others do not.

Learning doesn't always come from a workshop, book or official program however. You can and will learn many things over the course of career just by communicating with others. Your day-to-day interactions with colleagues and counterparts will fill you with much knowledge, and don't be afraid to ask a lot of questions. You can also job shadow and learn about other roles and departments within your organization. You might find this type of learning very interesting, even if it's not an endeavour that you want to pursue. It may just be about learning what others do in their roles, and how they keep the wheels turning. In an organization, all play a big part in the success of the company. I have often referred to it as a puzzle. If you're missing any part of this puzzle/roles, then you cannot be fully successful.

Whether you are the CEO or not, we all contribute in one form or another, and in many ways do more work as Assistants than some more senior roles. Don't ever let anybody make you feel like your role is unimportant. You are a crucial part of the puzzle, or you would not be needed.

Learning never exhausts the mind. — Leonardo da Vinci

CHAPTER 11
Virtually Hybrid (New Age)

Throughout my career as an Executive Assistant, I worked mainly onsite in an office environment Monday through Friday. That's approximately thirty-five years of commuting without the luxury of being able to work from home. Not only were there no laptops when I started my career, desktop computers were also a scarcity. Once all Administrators started getting a desktop computer, we were of course unable to take them home. It goes without saying that working from home as an Executive Assistant, or many other roles, was not only impossible but not even a thought at the time. Chatting with colleagues around the water cooler was a staple of our office experience, along with other more official interactions.

There is a lot to say about being onsite as an Executive Assistant. The comradery, communication and human interaction is very important, and something you cannot do as successfully when you work from home. That is my belief anyhow. There may be a feeling of isolation for some when not in an office environment as well, and for somebody who worked for so long in a historically 'normal' world, I don't mind the commute for various reasons.

I found that before the COVID-19 pandemic that only 20% of people who were able to work from home actually did so. As of 2022, that number grew to almost 60%. Perhaps even more depending on which country you live in. However, there are various cons to working from home. One aspect is that it can be difficult to differentiate / separate your work hours from your personal time. Some people work on their dining room table, then have dinner with their family in the same place. How about in-person collaboration?

You do not have that opportunity to do that when working from home either. There may be feelings of disconnection from your peers as well.

Having said that, there have been many pros to working from home that have not only aided us in continuing our administrative roles during the pandemic (not something many had the luxury of doing in other professions) but something we did not have much control over anyhow. As Executive Assistants we have learned to be even more flexible with our schedule and day-to-day work life. Without the extra time, effort and cost of commuting (more for some than others), we have adjusted to focusing more on our roles and managing our time more efficiently. This has given us the opportunity to be more in-tuned with our duties and responsibilities with less unforeseen interruptions. There's a lot to be said for having a quiet space to concentrate on the tasks at hand, seeing that most Executive Assistants do not have their own office outside the home. Even when I have had one, I often kept the door closed for less distractions.

Depending on the climate wherever you live, commuting may also be an inconvenience at times. When working from home you can dress 'somewhat' comfortably and still be effective, if not more so. The physical demands and dress codes that some companies have can make working from home ideal in that regard. The days of wearing suits and high heels to work are long gone, even for those who have been back to working onsite. Many companies have taken a more casual approach. But nothing like commuting on a bus, subway, train or car in the middle of a wintery day. Carrying all the requirements for your workday, and then slipping on an ice patch right before walking in your office front door. I'm not saying this happened to me but food for thought. These are all aspects that are not required when working from home.

There is also the financial savings aspect of working from home. The commute itself, clothes, food and of course childcare. In addition, various companies will reimburse you for in-home requirements for you to fully do your job outside the office (such as a laptop, desk, chair, mobile device, printer, etc.), as well as taxable deductions for utilities you use while working from home. The latter is usually covered by the government, or at least a percentage of it can be written off depending on where you reside.

A negative aspect I have experienced when working from home has been sick days, or lack of them. In this current hybrid world, if we are too sick to physically go into the office, we are sometimes questioned (or perhaps doubted) if we end up working from home; however, in the end we still commit to actually working from home and being online. Before the pandemic, if you called in sick you had to officially take a sick day. Unfortunate but a loss for both the employee and the company. The way I see it, we are still contributing from home even when we are unwell, which probably doesn't sit well for many people. For example, enduring food poisoning and still logging into your laptop to work from home, but receiving a snarky comment from your manager. Very unprofessional and offensive.

In the end there are pros and cons with hybrid situations but it also depends on who you ask. I personally enjoy the hybrid offering but was also very accustomed to working onsite full time for decades. I have conformed to the hybrid situation due to the pandemic and the repercussions it brought to numerous companies across the globe. I am comfortable working in either setting, and am grateful I am able to. There are many individuals outside the corporate world (i.e. first responders, tradespeople and couriers) who don't have that luxury. I commend them.

"Intelligence is the ability to adapt to change." – Stephen Hawking

CHAPTER 12
Glass Ceilings....and Floors (Gender Benders and Equality)

What does gender equality mean to you? Firstly, let's look at the basic definition of this. In a corporate setting, it's geared toward accessing the same resources and rewards, and having equal opportunities and pay. To me it is also about both genders having the same respect, no matter what your role or setting. This goes for any profession. Having said that, how many male Executives Assistants have you met? Are you a male Executive Assistant? I have met a few male Executives Assistants during my career but not many. Note that there are various administrative roles aside from an Executive Assistant, such as an Office Coordinator, Personal Assistant or Chief of Staff. With that, how many female executives have you met and/ or supported? Personally only approximately 20% of my bosses have been female, and although the overall percentage has grown over the past few decades, it's not nearly where it should be. Now I'm not the type of person to demand an equal leadership team solely based on gender but instead believe that only those who are qualified should be considered (male or female, administrative or executive).

The various male Executives Assistants that I researched have claimed that they "sort of fell into the role", as if to say that it wasn't their initial choice or goal. I'm not sure how to take that but most seemed to enjoy their careers regardless. Supporting a senior executive, politician or even a celebrity is a great responsibility, no matter what industry you work in. Although I cannot speak for everybody, I personally chose to be an Executive Assistant but did not start off as one. It took years of experience to earn that role and support C level executives.

Traditionally, the Executive Assistant role has typically been held by females. We *are* great multi-taskers by nature after all. However the various responsibilities of this career choice requires many facets and characteristic traits, whether male or female. Some people are just more suited for the role than others, no matter what your gender is. As a career administrator, I have been perturbed by those that ask, "where do you see yourself in five years" or "have you thought of going into a management position"? To me it's like asking a doctor if they would consider becoming a lawyer. The stereotypical mentality of 'just being a secretary' has not phased out as fast as I would have liked it to unfortunately but is improving. On the flip side however, most Executive Assistant job descriptions posted today by corporations require a university degree (or at least ten plus years of experience). This shows me that the prerequisites are there, therefore we should be considered professionals too – just like any other position.

So what exactly is a 'glass ceiling'? Basically this term is defined as the inability for women (or minorities) to be promoted (and I would include experience far less respect as well). Note that these inefficiencies have typically been invisible barriers and not anything a company would openly include in a corporate policy – not to say they were not real and not experienced by many. For some corporations, this metaphoric glass has been shattered and more women have been considered and respected in various types of roles, including Executive Assistants. How about the 'glass cliff'? This is a new one for me. As wrong and ludicrous as it may sound when we say it out loud, it's when women or those in a certain demographic are given promotions or senior opportunities knowing they will purposely fail (due to an expected but not known event or consequence). This way they can be blamed and dismissed without losing their prime candidates (or so in their own minds). We need to break this trend and mindset; however wrong and difficult it might be to prove it exists.

What I have found throughout my long career is that times have definitely changed, albeit somewhat slowly. I have experienced both ends of the spectrum, from a very condescending 'boys club' environment to more recently a very professional corporate setting, with the latter displaying more respect, inclusivity and diversity than in past years. Administrative roles have fought the good fight, and have come a long way but hoping all discriminatory actions (minor or not) will one day be eliminated. Whether related to hierarchy, age, race, gender or otherwise. Sometimes the 'powers that be' do not see our good intentions and dedication, and impose their inaccurate perspectives on us simply because they can. Speaking down to somebody in a corporate environment solely because you are superior (on paper) is basically a form of bullying. Don't let this happen to you and always speak up. Always! You must also know that I have actually met other Executive Assistants who they themselves displayed characteristics of discrimination, to myself and others. In my mind, this is totally unacceptable

In addition, Executive Assistants are moving away and forward from the traditional role, and no longer just take meeting minutes and manage calendars. We provide strategic business support, bring value in various ways, and have a positive impact on our leaders, teams and colleagues. We are influential as well, and an asset that AI (artificial intelligence) won't easily be able to replace – despite what some people might think.

Remember that just because you chose to become and remained a career Executive Assistant, it doesn't mean that you have conceded in any way and didn't want to advance in another role. Being a career EA is a respectable career, and has basically made me an expert, a specialist, a guru of sorts. Not to say that we ever stop learning, and don't ever let anybody discredit what you do. Break your own individual glass ceilings and reach for the stars! Whether male or female, you have the opportunity of doing great things and meeting wonderful people along the way. You will build lifelong connections, and maybe even form some good friendships.

"Injustice anywhere is a threat to justice everywhere." - Martin Luther King Jr.

CHAPTER 13
R-E-S-P-E-C-T (Recognition & Praise)

How often do you hear "thank you for all your hard work and dedication"? How often do you say this yourself to others? A kind word goes a long way. Hearing these words, when deserved, does much more than make us feel good. It motivates us to do even better. Studies have shown that just saying "thank you" or shaking somebody's hand in gratitude has a bigger impact than financial rewards.

But how do you get recognized? Doing your basic duties doesn't always guarantee this. Try showing off your skills, volunteer for new responsibilities, speak up about yourself (achievements, performance) and request feedback on a regular basis. Meet regularly with your leader and tell them how you feel, what you're working on, and what else you are capable of. Meet with other leaders as well. Many times, we report to one leader but support various other leaders. Ensure they too are aware of your capabilities, desires, and goals.

As of 2020, there were more than 1.8 million administrative professionals working in Canada alone. We have a great responsibility, and a great history in this country and around the world. We deserve to be recognized for our work, no less than any other position within a company. In fact, we have a whole week dedicated to celebrating us. Administrative Professionals Day. This observation started in the US in 1952 and has since been recognized in Canada and various other countries on the last week of April.

Admin professionals date back to the 15th century (and probably farther than that), with an increased demand in North America post World War II. In the 50s and 60s, most of these roles were filled by women, which to some extent is still the case today. With the influence and support of women's liberation groups in the 70s, we gained more respect in our roles and additional duties/training were implemented (i.e. Accounting). When computers started populating the workplace (which is when I entered the corporate world), our responsibilities increased immensely. For me personally, being an Executive Assistant has allowed me to wear various hats throughout my career, including Project Manager, Event Coordinator, Employee Communication, Photographer, Web Designer, etc.

How would you like to be recognized for the work you do? From a leader's perspective, there are various ways to recognize your Administrator. Invite them to lunch, recognize them at a meeting in front of their peers, give them a thoughtful gift or even a brief note of thanks. These are just a few ideas for recognizing an Administrator but unfortunately, in my experience, some companies/leaders never recognized me (nor other Executive Assistants) on this dedicated day – nor otherwise. I have even witnessed other team members receive recognition for work that I produced. This is not only very unprofessional but demeaning. Fortunately, this was not the case at every company I have worked at.

What if you have been tasked by your leader to recognize others? In the past, I have managed various initiatives to recognize individual colleagues and/or teams. This included contests, performance, and employee service. Contests were a great way to get all employees involved in any given initiative and recognize those who were most knowledgeable. This could have been centric to company history or another objective. Individual employee performance was also recognized for various reasons, whether related to on-time performance, results' oriented or teamwork history. Lastly, recognizing employees on their service award was always very fulfilling and many colleagues participated. What I found with any of these initiatives is that it engaged employees, motivated them, and all were very happy with their reward. It is no different in recognizing Administrators, whether for a milestone event or a daily, minor task.

Although we sometimes get overlooked amongst other staff, it should in no way reflect on our duty and the great responsibilities we have. Don't let this discourage you. Keep your head up high and continue doing the very best that you can do for the greater good. Some leaders are better than others at recognizing their staff, but it doesn't mean that you are not worthy of recognition.

How about praising your peers? Do you often say "thank you" to your colleagues? In most cases it doesn't take much to appreciate your co-workers. As an Executive Assistant, you often communicate with various individuals and teams on behalf of your leader, and you should always show appreciation – even for the little things. I have worked with many people who never give their thanks, while others you could always count on for some form of praise. Even for minor tasks.

Praise, recognition and rewards are very important to any organization. It uplifts morale and ensures employees are aware they are important and/or doing a great job. Some other points to remember are 1) be specific with recognition, 2) be timely, 3) highlight the impact of the situation, and 4) recognize amongst individual's peers. Most employees advise that regular recognition encourages them to do better. Therefore, imagine how it feels not to receive any. Also, there is some distinction between recognition and appreciation. One celebrates a specific event or milestone, while the latter focuses on an individual's value for how they are day-to-day. Both are important but different, nonetheless.

While various companies have internal performance award options (for recognizing colleagues), not all have this option. Those that do offer the opportunity for employees to praise each other, and even award points to those individuals. A point-based system is a great idea, especially for larger companies. But it still goes without saying that verbal praise is still the most effective, in my opinion, and goes a long way in recognizing your peers. From a simple 'thank you' to a focused speech during a team meeting. It is most rewarding for employees to hear praise, specifically from their leaders, amongst their peers. I would say it is the simplest and most effective.

"There are two things that people want more than money. Recognition and praise." – Mary Kay

CHAPTER 14
All Systems Go (Ongoing Technological Advancements)

Since the first day I saw a computer at my desk way back in the 80s, a lot has changed. With all the changes in technology, there is growth and you have to keep up with it. Anything related to your job, specific to your role or perhaps a software application that your team uses, I would suggest registering for some training.

When I first started working in an office environment, there were no computers. There was a typewriter and a lot of paper. Everything was processed manually, such as employee lists, accounting, overtime records, scheduling meetings, etc. There were also filing cabinets full of physical file folders. But soon after we started seeing desktop computers appear. After this, we started doing less and less things by pen and paper, and more and more on computers. However, we did keep our typewriters for the odd envelope we had to prepare (printers weren't that savvy for this back then either).

When I first studied computer science in college, it wasn't just software applications of that time and basic keyboarding. My program included all aspects of computers, including bits and bytes. We not only learned how to use a computer but how computers worked (inside and out). It gave me a better understanding of the technology. We gained knowledge on all capabilities of a computer and how we could best utilize them for our day to day tasks. In today's world, most people will purchase a laptop and merely follow all the steps to set up everything. Not sure if it's because I'm sort of a computer geek, but I think everybody should be trained on how a computer functions and not just how to use it.

When it comes to courses today on new software applications and advancements in existing software applications, I would suggest studying all of it. This way you are always current in your role, and it's for your own benefit. Not to mention, your company most likely encourages and pays for employee development. This way you're well educated and knowledgeable, and from the employer's perspective it's the same. They can feel confident knowing that you are well versed with all the technological advancements and that you can support them as required. Perhaps even programs your leaders are not familiar with. I would still suggest that all employees keep up with their training, including senior leaders – not just their Executive Assistants. In fact, a big part of my career I have helped senior leaders with the most minor technological requests because they did not know how to do it themselves. But this is part of our job, so it's more important that we always stay current.

Now most young adults are very savvy with technology, and were practically born with a laptop or tablet in their hand. Not to mention the infamous smartphone. We have all evolved in one way or another, and as it relates to being an Executive Assistant, our current technology has been a Godsend. Managing calendars, communicating with our leaders and others, holding virtual meetings, etc. These are extremely important aspects of our administrative roles that have been made more efficient due to technological advancement in our society. This has also enabled the typical Executive Assistant role to morph into something much more than the historical 'Secretary'.

The advantages of this new computer age isn't just about facilitating your job, although that is a big and very convenient advancement for Executive Assistants. We now have numerous ways of actually finding a job via the Internet, as opposed to reading a lot of newspaper ads, making various phone calls and dropping off resumes at companies in person or sending through the snail mail. We can peruse all the job postings online and research companies in advance in the simplest of ways. This may sound very trivial now, but trust me when I say it is such an amazing and efficient way to job hunt. From handing your resume to a recruiter, to faxing it across the country, to instantly sending it anywhere in the world in a blink of an eye. I understand that this may all go without saying to most, but I believe there are still a few of you out there who are not that computer savvy. In the very least, you have never used a recruiting website / process. What I can say is that you have many options to choose from, and a select few that target the most ideal jobs for you in your area the best. You can research these recruitment websites, which are all very easy to navigate, or you can ask somebody who has already used them for their own searches. If you are not very comfortable around a computer and/or English is not your first language, then I would suggest you take a beginner's course (in both computers and English) to help you advance your chances of having a satisfying and productive career as an Executive Assistant.

Another piece of advice for all new or upcoming Executive Assistants would be to have very professional and creative writing skills. This includes corporate etiquette and the best written mannerisms. As an Executive Assistant, it is a big part of your job to communicate with others – including various senior leaders (within and outside your organization). You must be as eloquent and accurate as possible, and relay your message (via email, letter or other format) in the most professional manner. Although most software applications for writing such communication provide spell checks and access to a thesaurus, it is up to you to ensure that your message is to the point. You should also consider the audience and who you are writing to. Most senior leaders do not want nor need a lengthy message, whereas HR might want more details of your story. Learn and keep up with technology, be/become a good writer, and perfect a new language or two. If you continue on a knowledge based path, you will exceed your own expectations.

"Any sufficiently advanced technology is indistinguishable from magic."
- Arthur C. Clarke

CHAPTER 15
It's Been a Slice (Resigning, Retiring)

Are you thinking of resigning? Stop and think about it for a moment. Do you have a plan in place? Do you have another job lined up already? Are there reasons you are planning on resigning? Are they negative reasons for resigning at your current company or just a better offer somewhere else? These are all questions you should ask yourself before you make any decision. If you're experience something in your current role that you're not comfortable with or perhaps even unsafe, you should speak with Human Resources first. Ironically enough, I've been with companies where either the issue was with my manager and/or Human Resources themselves. Needless to say I resigned from those companies due to their toxic environments. What was even more interesting is that the individuals in these roles were ultimately dismissed from said companies some time after I had resigned. I suppose everything happens for a reason. The important person in these scenarios is you! Don't ever feel pressured to stay nor feel bad for resigning. You are your number one priority, and if you have your solid reasons for leaving a company, then be confident about your decision and stand your ground. They will eventually fill the role you leave behind, and you will be happy in your new situation.

Whatever your reasons for leaving a company, always leave on a good note. You don't want to burn any bridges. What this means is you are professional with your resignation, you give two weeks' notice, and you do your work respectfully until your last day of employment with that company. You don't want to be unprofessional with your current boss or other employees, and then come across them at another company. You might also want to attain good references from your current employer, so it's best to leave that company in a good light and by the book. Even if you're not happy with a situation or individual, keep it professional as you exit.

Another thing to think about is do you really want to leave your current employer, and if so, why? Make sure you have solid reasons for resigning and that you are not just upset over one small incident that can otherwise be resolved easily. Don't be hasty in your decision. Take some time to think about it. One bad day at work doesn't warrant resigning from a company. Although Executive Assistants have many options in their career, building experience within the same company for an extended period of time is beneficial. However, if you've experienced the same negativity for six months, for example, and are still not happy about it with no changes in site, then it's probably time to move on. There is absolutely no place for abuse, lack of advancement or disrespect. And you don't owe anybody an explanation when you decide to resign, except that you are advancing your career elsewhere. Just remember that we all have good and bad days wherever we are employed, so try to gauge the situation and what is best for your future.

If not resigning, are you possibly nearing the age of retirement? If you're reading this book, you may not be nearing retirement – or perhaps you are retired already and just interested in my story (which would be nice). But if you're younger, and probably not thinking much about it, you should be. That's one thing I would have told my younger self. At my age, although not retired yet, it's something I think about now. I want to be prepared when I *do* end up retiring and have some savings, investments, etc. on-hand and ready for that transition. Most companies offer investment options as a benefit, and some even make contribution matches to your investments (up to a certain percentage). It's basically free money, so why not? Retirement is something you would speak to your manager or Human Resources about, and learn any stipulations on timing and benefits well beforehand. If you work for a larger company, you will find detailed information on retirement on their employee Intranet site. This should include all the information and forms you might require for your retirement. You can also check government websites and see what and when you are entitled to retirement funds and pensions. They will also have minimum age requirements and other rules laid out for you to read. Depending on your current age, you may be able to already start applying for those benefits now. As well, some websites have retirement calculators that you can use (at any age) to get an estimate on what you will be entitled to when you do retire, even if it's not imminent.

What if you're not quite ready to retire as an Executive Assistant, or really any other position but you're approaching the age of retirement? Do you want to officially retire from your current company now but still work later, perhaps in a part time capacity (at existing company or elsewhere). Do you want to work longer at your current company. Is that permitted? What if you want to retire now but be a freelance Executive Assistant. With so many virtual options available to you, being a contracted administrator might be an ideal opportunity for you. You can work on a consultant basis or just temp work based on your desire to continue working. Remember, when you are a career Administrator and all your experience becomes your forte, you can easily find opportunities like these and choose to work from home or at a local office. It's all up to you and your choice to make.

At the end of the day, you don't want to enter into your retirement stage with any preconceived notions or concerns. You want to be prepared, healthy and happy. If you're in a position to fully retire and do other things, such as traveling, then that's what you will do. If you want to continue as an Executive Assistant and help support others for a bit longer, than you can do that instead. Look forward to both a fulfilling career and retirement.

"Retirement is the world's longest coffee break. Enjoy your coffee!
"

CHAPTER 16
Famous Last Words (In Closing)

I'm not sure how famous my last words will be here but if you've made it this far, I hope I've given you some realistic, friendly and helpful advice for your career as an Executive Assistant. Based on my personal experience, being an Executive Assistant has been a very rewarding career with many ups and downs but if I wasn't always smiling, I was learning and becoming more knowledgeable. I have always tried to be humble and respectful, and hope those that I have supported were able to see that during my time with them.

No matter where life takes you as an Administrator, whether you're an Executive/Personal Assistant, Office Manager or Chief of Staff, be proud of yourself and be patient. All good things come to those who wait. I myself didn't start my career as an Executive Assistant. It took time and experience. And now there are multiple prerequisites on administrative job descriptions, including university degrees – unless you have ten or more years of experience. Again, continue your education throughout your career. Most colleges and universities throughout North America, and beyond, have dedicated programs for office administration because it's not all about handwriting letters anymore and hasn't been for quite some time. Don't ever be ashamed of starting off in a junior role. You will get to where you want to be and will be happy when you do.

Don't be discouraged when you first start out as a junior administrator. When I first started my career, I didn't have a mentor as related to my role. For decades I did it on my own and kept persevering. But about two to three years ago, something strange happened. Younger Executive Assistants started approaching me for advice. They asked all sorts of questions, ranging from procedural concerns to my advice on their own careers. I came to the realization that I became the mentor. It was a very humbling moment in my career, and I was tickled pink to help them in any way I could – and continue to do so. Just one of the reasons I decided to write this book. I wanted to encourage others to pursue their administrative careers with pride and knowledge, and know that you can be very successful depending on where your path leads you. I wanted to share my honest opinions and experiences with you, something I didn't have myself. I am where I am today because I *did* continue my studies, because I *did* stay in some jobs that I wasn't fully content in, and because I *did* rise above all that and became successful. I worked for some amazing companies, and with some amazing people. I raised my family and have had a career I thoroughly enjoy.

I have met and worked with some very good people throughout my career as an Executive Assistant, and overall still work with some amazing individuals. You get to build some very positive relationships, and personal friendships. People who I worked with decades ago that still keep in touch, leaders and counterparts. It is comforting to know that I made an impact on those I worked alongside or supported, and that they too made an impact on me.

I want you to strive to be the best that you can be, as an Administrator and otherwise. Never give up! I hope you get all the roles that you deserve and try to never settle. As you progress throughout your career, you will be able to be more selective as time goes by. The more experience you have, the easier it will be. I have met Executive Assistants from all over the world. Some who support very senior executives in various industries, including aviation, music, financial and technology, who I still communicate with. From Europe to Asia, and all across North America. It's good company to be in and to keep the door open. I hope you too build relationships with other Administrators and share ideas and strategies with them. Always be respectful, and expect respect in return as well.

Continue your education, and work on all your technical kills. Remember that all your soft skills will come very naturally to you in the workplace too because these are skills you already have in your personal life. Whether you are very organized at home and/or have a growing family, these traits will be beneficial in an office environment. Just try to keep a line between being organized with your children and being organized with your leaders. The intent will be similar but communication must be at an obvious different level. I've experienced some individuals who speak with their leaders and peers like they do with their children. This is not acceptable.

And if you are working in a toxic environment or are not happy for any other reason, the decision to move on is yours. Discuss it with your partner, another family member or a good friend if you want some objective feedback. But always have a backup plan and be well prepared for the move. Communication is key, and can in most cases resolve various issues. Don't be hesitant to speak with somebody about it. This might be your best course action before deciding to resign. But if you do decide to call it quits, remember not to burn any bridges. You want good references, and the good relationships to continue.

I wish you much success for the future in all that you endeavour to do and whichever path you decide to take. In the end, it's up to you if and when you should change that path. There is always more than one direction to take. Just ensure you are comfortable with your decision.

Good luck to all present and future Executive Assistants out there!! Thank you for listening.

"Success isn't about the money you make but the difference you make in people's lives." Michelle Obama

BIO

I am the daughter of Portuguese immigrants, who along with my brother first came to Canada in the early 60s. My parents worked and studied very hard to give us a good life in Canada and I thankfully inherited that work ethic myself. I was born and raised in vibrant Toronto, Ontario, Canada, where I have lived and raised a family in its central and suburb communities. I have three wonderful adult children, as well as two lovely granddaughters. I also have a very supportive husband, who continuously encourages me to do better, and is always there with not only his genuine guidance but with his humourous demeaner.

Shortly after completing my formal education, where I attained my 'Word Processing' diploma, I started my career as an Administrator in the mid-80s. As I slowly climbed the corporate ladder, my various titles also started to change and become more senior. This was due to varying factors but mostly because of my increased knowledge and continuing education. I have worked in various industries throughout my career, and as my personal soft skills were being sharpened, my business skills were also improving. I truly believe that the two go hand-in-hand.

Over the years I attended various administrative conferences, workshops, and training programs in order to stay current. In 2018 I received my ACEA designation (Advanced Certificate Executive Assistant) in London, England, and since then became a certified Specialist in various Microsoft Office applications (namely Word, Excel, Outlook and PowerPoint). I continue my educational path at every opportunity, and encourage you to do the same. I have also attained certification in other industries / roles, such as a certified

Access Control Officer and as an AAM (Aviation & Aerospace Manager) with the Canadian Counsel of Aviation & Aerospace.

On a more personal note, I have volunteered hands-on with various charitable organizations, including but not limited to Second Harvest, the Starlight Foundation, the Pinball Clemens Foundation, the MLSE Team Challenge and the Rally for Kids. I have also attended various charitable functions as an ambassador on behalf of companies I was representing, which I thoroughly enjoyed and found very fulfilling. There is nothing better than giving back to the community when and wherever you can. A few other honourable mentions – I used to ride a motorcycle, have traveled the world, love to oil paint and photography, and recently swam with dolphins. Needless to say my life has and continues to be quite rich.

My inspiration for writing this book was to share my vast career history so that others will have a realistic perspective on what it's like to be, become and succeed as an Executive Assistant, which has been my official title in most recent years. I discuss various topics, including education, job offers, equality, harassment and technological advancements. These and many more will all consistently play a role in your career, and I hope yours is very prosperous and successful.

Thank you

Ana Maria Dorevich (née Monteiro)

LET'S TAKE THIS OFFLINE

Copyright 2024, Author A. Dorevich